# THE LIE
# NEAREST TRUTH

# THE LIE
# NEAREST TRUTH

POEMS

SEAN GARRITTY

The Sheep Meadow Press
Rhinebeck, New York

Designed and typeset by The Sheep Meadow Press.
Distributed by The University Press of New England.

All inquiries and permission requests should be addressed
to the publisher:

The Sheep Meadow Press
P.O. Box 84
Rhinebeck, NY 12572

Library of Congress Cataloging-in-Publication Data

Garritty, Sean.
 The lie nearest truth / by Sean Garritty.
   p. cm.
 ISBN 978-1-931357-87-6 (pbk. : alk. paper)
 I. Title.
 PS3607.A77375L54 2011
 811'.6--dc23

                          2011048396

## WITH GRATITUDE

I would like to thank my parents, family, and friends for their support over the years. I would also like to acknowledge my teachers and colleagues at the University of Alberta and Brooklyn College—many of the poems in this book have benefitted from your insights and care. Thank you to Peter for your love and support and your keen, exacting eye on matters of design. And, particularly, thank you to Stanley Moss for your amazing contribution to poetry in the last sixty years, least of all this small book.

## ACKNOWLEDGEMENTS

Poems in this volume have previously appeared in *The Olive Reading Series Chapbook.*

Author photograph by Tyler Grant.

# CONTENTS

# 1

2

# THE LIE
# NEAREST TRUTH

# 1

# THE LIE NEAREST TRUTH

This *is* living—but too, too convincing,
the humdrum spectacular

leaving some bar, head wombed,
floating along with the aural flotsam

with hands held in a sticky promise
not like the handjob in Elizabeth, New Jersey.

In a dream there is a naked teenager surrounded
by sketch men all for beauty and ugliness.

Morning's enigma machinery—come agaïn—
like silkscreens, unique yet exactly the same,

it takes so much to mine the infrathin allowance—
the prescriptions of post-minor surgery

better a stiff drink, or a little courage—
weightlessly delicate in its off-putting celibacy.

There is no truth, so we must lie.  Near
as a boy under the skin like a terrible infant

the loathe platitude of figuring it out,
as unconvincing as a life already lived,

an awake state at that specious hour:
when is it late, when is it early?

## COLD, HUNGRY & DRY

Patron of a swollen river
not like the immobile muck of muck

wander across a country
and dig your ribs in a curve of city

the hobo logic of punks and wolves
that it's okay to cross

not the avenue one lane too wide
hey, I've been there and you, you're so tough

all thumbs, the least superfluous digit
except that there's two of 'em

whiskeys in their glad rags, flip a boho nickel
they still speak from an other,

content in a silk bindlestick
a beer foam of language

think of all the slang we've yet to learn
all the secrets we get to dress up

in charcoal steam eye shadow
a spot of blood on each cheeked bone

railing down valley, down stairs
wear swish at the hip

everything's gesture, misfits look
at each other as much as they're looked at

as strong an embrace, but bound
to fail up to annihilation

put it down and call it a paper victory
a crumpled tissue to bundle this mess

# A FANCIED DEATH IN THE COLD

A pink almond branch
snowed in a muddled palette—
this road is a little too precious.
But there it is, at my eyes.

It isn't black ice,
a distraction-led car crash
of steel and pink snow,
the radio's phlegmy *Black Coffee*.

The tires still move
and we go nowhere,
a wheel to the shoulder,
sick fumes in cold air

that will kill me, will kill
my imagination,
this wintering zoo
of pink fox and snow,

that even now the mind wanders,
the machinations of shock
and small weaknesses and
a small deal of time.

The star lights are a shining city.
I can hear white noise pink
in the fading Sunday.
The battery dies to the radio

and a flickering dash.
There's a depression in the steel
which fits my collapsed frame
in the cold—this fancied death.

SLOW POKE


Can you tell I was a blonde child,
see the lump of the wrist bone suggests *what if*,
as if meant for other weights, other arms.

Hey squirt, it isn't that funny,
just a new axis to pull and pivot,
you needn't a drastic flexibility

but a glass eye to see in as out.
That would help, to be helped.
No one will help.  Underexposed

length of the bone to wrist,
it's too late to unravel the fade and curl
of film left to shadowed light.

Wait, wait, wait,
some cute kid in the mirror eyes.

AGONY AUNT


Condensation on the cooling hot egg cup,
a slurry of yolk waits to be cracked

        and you've chosen now

to feign a Death of Marat expression
a moment before swallowing hard back,

        an interstitial gesture

that awakes between a thought and its mouthing—
I never could see my own expression, though

        with imagination...

no—here, memory will suffice—
there was that crackled oil on panel

        some near-east baron

red-eyed with the long flash of history.
You're saying, *advise me.* Breakfast just got soggy.

        With nothing to use

what sugared invention
am I expected to bring to syrup?

# LIE DETECTOR TEST

I notice,
the lessoned pulse
an unreflexive pupil—
you're so good at this.

Meanwhile,
I'm speaking to your cheekbones,
my hands intimate
with every object at grasp.

Grüner Veltliner,
that's—what—my fifth now?
Read the subtext:
a cigarette, a cloud.

Admittedly,
you've beat the machine.
The shaker knocked salt
oh yes, check *please.*

## STARING CONTEST

Listful silence attends
us double voyeurs'
each bat lash.
A few off-pigments weak,
you as collected
as a breathless statue

in a sexualized light,
its always-movement
a whoring bee to a flower,
to a flower, to a flower.

The westerly sun
is a casual onlooker
we recognize and choose
to allow its witness
of a witness of a witness.

A dusty headache
forming at your temple—
I am allowed to wonder,
is it me or the silence,
the witness or our light?

Whatever the gloss
on my eyes may ask,
please don't answer.
I'm more interested in the question.

# TONIGHT, TO MORNING

For at least this morning
you are *My baby!* to a burning building,
dawn a thin line of lubricant
down my inseam descent,
lines of cotton and the wall clock
are tickertape, and cat eyes will be me,
a reckless, skeptical gaze.
These are the players.

> *It's just a wishful thought*
> *to want an exeunt severally,*
> *such casual direction allowing*
> *the actors a measure of freedom.*
> *But I'm dreaming a soliloquy*
> *not even an audience will espy.*

Now I am this sticky, adult body.
Once again, it has reclaimed me.
Yet something of my disposition
remains a Celan poem, even to me,
and you are some other language
I'm eager to learn.

PERJURY


The papers are signed. Hold me,
just not to anything
like daytime sun to the evening light,

or the legalese of holding another's hand.
I found my certainty
was written in invisible inks

the sort of absence-presence stuff
a philosophy student might extol,
but which pulls my wheel hand dangerously left.

Now I wait for the sun's bleaching warmth
as beyond white the snow will melt
nearest lies to be purged.

## MS. HIGHSMITH

It starts with a brief martini lunch
and I will work barefoot, in my Levis,

my shirtsleeves, then each successive button
will allow the sun my shoulders

and our murders of this large small continent,
your garrote, my skulling stone

and with the disposal we get creative.
Was it this real for you? Because I'm sweating.

Yes, Pat, you may borrow my keys
so long as they unlock for you

but will you introduce me to your anti-hero,
introducing me as your anti-villain?

Neither of us is a failed mystery writer,
that joke's funny now we've hit the bottle.

It gets difficult to see the writing, like a murderer
not knowing what his hands accomplish emotionless

or in a feast of emotion, in the embracing
of words as culpable as deeds.

# THE UNICORN IN CAPTIVITY

It is enough to say, 'the beast is captive,
if not by the toyish fence than,
why not? by the very fabric.'
It is weft in the weave

as are a clutch of plump, red seeds
sluicing violets and age rot
on the wall, not to be trampled
as a summer idyll.

You prefer this eternally deferred escape,
its nose to the pigment, this more often
hotel room print with its
eyes of some dozen stitches.

This is what you get bumming off
cigarettes, a school tour,
a chill afternoon on Dyckman street
at the foot of the Cloisters.

# ICE CUBES SO RARELY ARE


He settled in as a lesser Romanian vampire,
we can't all be the well-situated eutactic star thing.

Casual thirst takes on an other-real shape
but there isn't a name for it

especially when he no longer wants
what he wants. But still…thirsty thirsty.

The turnoffs are plain enough, tumorous adam's apples,
the stinging particulars of a drugstore eau

and the ever-predictable struggle for life
(even in the arms of one so handsome—
          really, it's the way to go).

A crumpled tuxedo nap, the moment before
a murky Rhone spills another carpet stain to the floor:

his blood thins.  It's not what he is, he thinks,
but what he became.

JAMAIS VU

Afferent efferent, and each
counterpoint is ellipsed,
*try saying "insouciance"*
*with a little more* oomph.

First sight always questions,
you see: his look asks
and words form at the mouth,
say a name again again again with
meaning lost or its establishment.

Now you're reading aloud on the subway
but I just can't picture the daffodils
over the brass of a demon aria.

A Dervish in a staring contest gets carsick,
pupil dark a still never seen.
Who floats through such moist air
and still sees—possibility?

I can already tell you will try
to see in the dark, seek to touch
the deathly silence of winter.
I might too but a headache's coming on,
this Faustian deal of head-cold for a kiss.

NOVELETTE

They're liked, just twee markings
and foxing marginalia

cupped hands at eyes like
that lemon yellow limelight

an intoxicant as even the most
dull wishbones may be

this is all to say, this is all to say,
a second chance at a first chance

a scratch on the record
that somehow makes pretty

as it revolves, as you turn
you're my newest lovely old book

and on second reading, I know
you will be read, and read, and read.

FLOTSAM


I stand watch as the tide goes out.
Returning, it will not contain you.

I thought of you as that which remains
when the ship's long sunk,

that there was enough in sea air
to sustain a minor life.

Now I keep words like bottles of sea
alone from water.

I myself cannot float:
I thought you enough for us both

and I'm not holding my breath
for a few lengths of sea foam and jetsam.

# THIEVES' CANT

There is a way of saying something,
hints of blue tint and so

haves and needs, passions and fashions
all clearly eluded just so.

All clearly eluded but in clearless
backhandness says, but is it so?

Whatever he is, whatever he says,
I hear it he says he is so.

A sad song and a side glance,
just as he says will be so.

DEFENSE

My soft Champagne bubble
on the rise then pop

like a good egg from East Egg,
the past excels at catch-up

though it is not mine,
I am free to admire

your crestfall
the traject of my own self

delayed by sand in my shoes,
wishy wash and whatnots

twee anecdotes with
fierce consequences

this is my defense of nostalgia
of non-experience

so we all live on islands:
so what's yours is mine.

# THE OTHER SIDE OF A WINDOW

*1.*

The window of espial is an empty reflection by day
but reveals, in its false contents' absence, when the day falls,
and after many, many days.

I knew it was safe, yet crept like the smaller gender
of a spider species, the one with weaker bite,
and the black window was not difficult to pry.

An ineffable scent filled the air and drenched his pillow
where I rested my head, analyzing,
and his bedroom from a new perspective.

From where I lay, the shrill view
of my own window through his caught me,
and they talk of experiencing another's skin.

He gave me no choice.
I gave the very glance I had been waiting for,
and if I was only there to see it.


*2. A turn of phrase*

Him in front
of a mirrored glass, small
stale cold war—as different as apples
and apples behind a plane of glass.
An arms race, a torso race, a whole city watching itself.

The voyeur    alone, surrounded
              hungry, full, filled
              touches with eyes

                    "This is just a test"
                    is a colossal disappointment
                    when the eyes can't see
                    the piercing howl.

Stop thinking of the pupil
as ink in an inkwell,
it isn't worth it.

                    Lowest common denominator,
                    we see what we believe.

# WAKES, VOICED AND SILENT

it's about time
the river collected its winter ice

in a slipstream
dream thrives on restless fever

sustaining, sustained
by its own, only heat

a year's progress measured in yards
days, and days

leaves turn and hide
in a mint-cool window

I'm searching for the optimist's side
of a man half-drowned


*your watch long dead*

*well, the train's gone anyway*

*the men are pickaxing*

*at metal, stone*

*yes, a door opens a door*

*alive as mote dust sun*

*everything says give up*

*to the small heat inside*

NIGHT IN ST. CLOUD


Wet dust of steam,
wood polish, rail polish and
closer still, a haze of camphor on boiled wool.
The flaneur now watched, shoegazing.

The crowd is a grand, needless whisper:
the other side of the room
on the other side of the room.

*Soon enough, soon enough.*

PULL

This that is warned against,
attacks of the heart and sore livers

scarred flesh and stretched to vellum.
It makes for weak tea.

I'm cutting through the scroll
for codex materials,

at very least the work is useful,
a day of words in a field of tired silence.

What an act of poet, I accept
my own gestures as theatrical, if reserved.

You can't be the first at any thing, any more
than you can invent gravity

so in some sense I feel better,
an askew poet on Tudorian television

who is read,
though not remembered,
though read.

# HARD TIMES PARTY HARD

Victorian tarts hail hansom cabs
with delicate contumely,

chiefly, my interest lies
in the slangs and smooth skin

a kerfuffle of shifting linens
and the slight sleight goings on

of the alley off the alley
in a darkly lit SoHo

or under a towering bridge
near weeds knee high.

Hoof it when the trains shut down
though the streets twine

as if lost in embrace,
so we'll keep our destination vague.

Nothing to get to anyway,
and no thing worth escaping.

# WEATHERING

*1.*

You can't trust anyone
until they've seen you through
and through a winter—and yet,
I know those who survive
in a seasonless warmth,
unwanting of a seachange
no solstice will ever announce.

I suppose I expect more
of the cold moon sun,
snow flowers,
and the toll of weathering.

*2.*

Late spring, the air begins to smell
of children's cereal.
I tilt my head toward the sun:
erratic stones, melting and left behind.

Beneath my feet the pavement
cracks, but holds.

TENSE

The choicest are always present
but the libration must be patterned

various petroleum of artistic youth
stuck around in a hazy air

scuffed knees and knife slips,
they are scars not memories

his pale leg descending into a gym short
a moment my youth in present tense

it is seductive *now*,
the past is just legs and paint fumes

the bloom of this one evening
now petals in our dead nature.

# 2

INFATUATE


It was that afternoon we had decided
our own exquisite particulars,
yours something of a boho curlicue,
an intimate weave of Django guitar,
fortified wines and safe cigarettes.
We were in Paris.  Perhaps, Trieste.
And somehow it thrived for me.

Somewhere down the line, we had taken the train
out east, I was flirting with a sort
of brown fascism, while
your eyes splashed blue
on the cliff of your cheek
and the moog vibe simply radiated
off the razored wall:
we were smeared across
a glossy magazine spread.

What we had missed
that afternoon, in your old basement
was the swamp carpeting, lying around
in our underpants with the bare
hiss of the record player,
more film cell than teenage prison.
And while dreaming up our ideal aesthetic,
we were already living it.

# BRETAGNE

The odd accoutrement of a misspent youth
rapt in cinema, the heat barely escaping

from stray alley to the untried sea.
It was the doctor's thinking, the lengthy train,

our brash argot awash in the raised-collar
air of an inrush morning

overripe citrus in the sea-fields,
finding even oysters to steal, tasting

like the discovery of parent's hiding places,
the few final slurps of childhood.

CANOPIED


Thousands of caterpillars draping a ravine,
a supernumerous existence
descent on silk, spiderly—
as if once in a decade, the end
or beginning of a long cycle,
they demand an audience.
They sour the path
and the wind through the web
pays a noisome tribute
to the curled leaves, clung like trash.

A soft caress, like their soft coil
down a boy's neck,
takes me away, in all ways.
But the inevitable flourish allowed to burst
is a paperful of imagination
put aside by spray or frost.
What lies in the mind
that did barely exist.

covering neatly
or entirely messy

a farmer's line of ash
or a forested den

foundlings bound in silk
or reposed mid air

thousands of caterpillars
or are they insects still

when metamorphosing
or dying in early frost

following a crumbling path
or barely a creek

was it going lost
or gone pell mell

under years of rot
or veils of leaf

a pale boy
or never to be kept

it was forgettable and a long way off

37

there were trees and there was silk

things got messy

## FAT RILEY

Fat Riley, there's no skinny boy
inside you somewhere,
hiding like you
in that tall-grass field.

What's done there, or
what had you found there, I
can't recall, or you
never told anyone.

*I'm a small creature,*
*a few nerves alone*
*handle my pain.*

Some adult said,
*...then the barking stopped.*
*Our son lit the fire.*

Then it's all over town,
what officials dug up,
a whole season used up—
summer unfolded like a Murphy bed
in a summer home.

There was some belief
but everyone wondered,
*do I feel it in my bones?*

I know what you said,
*life's a fifteen second riddle*
*the rest of you*
*never bother to solve*

and I felt it everywhere.

## A MORNING MINDFUL

Early still in Daguerre Wood,
it took moments for the eye to pull
enough image from the earthy
shadow covering the forest floor.
Only the odd trace of light rust
managed through the canopy above.
He contemplated the thought that he
wanted it this way,
vague texture of a lonely path stone,
blurred flush of skin, forest patina,
a felled tree slowly presenting itself to the soil.

All morning there, very little said.  Just
*You will, because that is what we both want.*

All seemed positioned,
and when the rain came, it too behaved
like a well-plotted sentence.  Hovering
under the nearest awning, next to
an afternoon of tavern men, stale quiet
just on the other side of a recessed door, waiting
for the hot rush of alluring tavern smell
when the sober stepped in or
the maudlin stumbled out.

JASPER

That night at that cabin, when I knocked the leeks
simmering in olive oil and butter to the floor:

sometimes you cannot start over, more often
it seems more useful to get to the end of things.
And all that time spent navigating their dense architecture,
careful for the odd grain of sand or soil—what of that
incubating soup, it was simple and fresh.

Maybe whiskey gives its own kind of awareness,
    *can you remember*
the dancing hand gestures that seemed
to ask not reveal.  Was the wine sweet or dry,
or neither in our sweet, dry mouths drunk on mountain air.

*Tell you what—no, tell me what*
because a mountain still has a certain gravity
and I wonder if gravity
is the only thing we might truly experience
so smooth and instantaneous and invisible
like the mountain hiding in a real darkness.
See how the two things become inseparable.

Elaboration is a good way of living, I think
even then I knew this without realizing it.
And even if we truly are just a handful of pale magnets,
repelling towards and against our desires,
how comforting to realize
there are some things a slope can't slide.

## FUN HOUSE NARCISSUS

In any case, if you stare long enough
you'll see whatever you wanted
but not what you want because no one sees
ahead, looking straight ahead but
looking down.  Your eyes become grey-green,
like the canals of Venice, your pupils a bat
skirting wildly over the surface, looking
for a capture but creating its escape,
a game played only with one's self.
You can almost hear the surface warp and
then collapse, and the collapse is the
    continuing warp,
and you forget which eye is looking at which eye.
They call acts like this time-honoured, and it
is always time at heart, the heart alone
and sightless in its cage and casually dictating.
You think nothing with your heart, you think
with your eyes barely understanding what you see.
Yours' is the face you understand least, so
why not give a little time to its gestures
now that its beauty is gone and the reflection
matters more and less, ebbing and flowing
with desire and reality.  In a better version,
you'll get so close as to kiss the mouth
and drown without gasping, alone and never alone.
Now you're seeing things my way.

# THE DUNCE CAP

The world is round without a corner
then I manage to find one,
something to finally put my back into
and the Goya looks down on me
in its own self-reflexive inquisition.

The point is, what better place to inquire
of the observance of humanity
than from the pedestal, on view.
My baldness hidden, I am comfortable
with the display and displaying.

It's how we treat our most revered
works of art, our fallen leaders and followers,
a collection of fruit and flesh,
with a small allowance of height
and the warmth of our eyes.

I'm making friends with my own stupidity.

# AVOIR TROIS MÉTROS DE RETARD

*to Jean Rhys*


For those women
you thought

drunk on stationery
and your Remington portable

the faint rush of the Seine
in the distance, my hard drive

with words snuck in
like a man into your boarding house

so here we are, now
at that point of night
between the dog and the wolf

I have crushed the ice

this drink is for you
and the life
I barely missed

PASTICHE LITE


The leaves are green.
Really they are white
because there is enough
light, that no mere object
could pull favourites.

One does not see
pitch black as one
does not see
an eyelid's verso,
its concavity,
but for staring at the sun
but not staring for the lids
are closed
and that it is not too wise.

     Prints of Geurnica
                    are Geurnica

And those
who only knew
red as fresh blood
might see it blue
at the instant
of its letting,
rare moments
of pure light.

In the hyperbolic
the minute, the dance

of whiter water or
bluer ice
all cannot help
but slow down
as everything slows down
like light bending
down the drain.

*Yet the weeks slip by,*
*never really there*

    *just seen*

# I'M WALKING FOR SLEEP

Q: *We've had our share of restless nights?*
A: (the bedclothes didn't argue)

It's about time the waves slow down I get up
and sleep-search my bed
for some thing soon forgotten
like the plot of not-quite-dream.
It's worrying: one day
that some thing might actually be there
to find, and affirming this state
I would neither wake up nor fall down
at the foot of true sleep's bed.
My body asks so little,
who would I be to not submit,
instead the gift of a cold shoulder
to a peculiar, circadian longing,
like a clergyman taking his vow
of celibacy, dis-
missing his wet dreams
and keeping his sheets stiff
with the coarsest,
most granular of detergents.
Of all fears why this?
Having taken on most fears
I take our sleep for more
than a lower brain wave—
enough of what matters
is tucked and locked away,
compartments of memory,
diminutive apothecary drawers,
the sticky geometry of honeycomb.

47

So I "live" a little less
(sleeping it off for sleep's sake)
but this is still a life
and it's doubtful there's much to miss
except that experience
might recharge those few morning hours
when life is only mine
with a few worthy memories,
for a respite from what they call living.

LEAST SINCERE


*It was a tingling in the brain,*
*which started from the awareness*
*of only having to stretch out one's hand.*

I never wanted to go to bed
so I read Frank O'Hara poems to pretend
he kept me awake.

Listen Sebastian, each of us chooses our own arrow.

Some study ice flows, or Manhattan schist.
On the corner, this man made in the
        delicious combination
of Ivy League and grime white t-shirt studied sewers
polluting the baseline with petroleum.
Me, I'm thinking
                *... baseline...Vaseline...*

but quitting before things start – it seems
the scapegoats learned to lawyer up,
for instance pomegranates are useless
now in poems, yet I muddle the padded seeds
with bourbon and crushed ice and my poem gets going.

Five minutes in a stalled subway car,
it can feel like five full tries
at an Earth's rotation, and I'm feeling flushed
but knowing a fever is just a trick
the body pulls on the invasion,
I'm hoping this fast one won't last.

I Scratched: *you are never the less*
*a comet, what they would call a hairy star*
*white as a peacock frozen in a winter zoo*
*seeing invisibility for all its 'I's.*

(You'll notice these are unfit ideas, though
when writing poems it is always useful to think
of cold, white space)

A neighbor: "I tense and blue," but on the inside
like breath digesting in her belly.
Everyone else: *what is this patience of geology?*

Still waiting, I read a magazine article with little more
than what I comprehend most, that I can't believe
what we want to believe.

SHEEP

A following fan-blade cuts another's air
yet is of the same object, the same motion:
history will say we never saw things the same way.
Somewhere in a field, large but south
of the Chandrasekhar Limit, you said

              *otherwise*
        *seems all good*
      and later

*anything that can be counted can at least be held.*
*Once the math was still new, but even then*
*limits were only so as concepts.  Now we believe it.*

      I told you

*The radio had made a contest out of burying*
*a gold bar for that summer's listeners.*
*I was pleased for I was made to think*
*of all that drove this town in the beginning,*
*the beaver pelts and the scattered pellets*
*of gold that might take years to fill out*
*an ingot, each one, its own version of the bar.*

A vague wave through the wild grass
like a silhouette of the years
that only follow old years.

*At birth and from it*
*our feet were already wet:*
*it's a typical day.*

Who said that?

NEW PIGMENT


There was a gentle, forceful drawing out

a warm curve of armpit
        bergamot scent, scant
on the skin, tinged with plum shadow
and green caress

Procrustean grips
on your narrow frame like
a handful of skeleton keys

and the steep
hull-wood of your torso
sunk in a perverted dirge
to a life so profoundly coloured,
captured    my darling,
                    darjeeling

# SOIRÉES 100% ROCK

SOIRÉES 100% ROCK, that is
a quiver in the throat like
the L running el
in all its steely aplomb,
the night and they caught by
its curve like a long arm.
Railings are worn reflective,

gimlet eyes absorb saloons
and the dust of our 100 years
Phew! for moisture
and an under-lamp light
where blue and red do not purple.
When our goat will be got
we will learn.

# WAS THE YEAR STILL NEW?

Remember when we picked
up on killing decisions—
January haunting our nights
like an 1813 winter—
and up to let days fall
where they may.
Ravens held their wings
embracing streetlights,
hiding the daylight
to keep them warm
so we thought       why bother
when some small details are enough,
(all things worse as precursors)
or we could be asleep:
essentially, the yellow morning
our resolve and worth matched.

## THE AMSELFLUH

So long
        as the tool will pierce you,
a horn or a pistol,
it doesn't make much a difference.
The avalanches were terrible that season
but when they settled,
scavengers like us had a field day.
The gradient of a pink slope
is often unmappable
and should instead be circumvented
to avoid seeming
like a brash tough or thug
because that's what it's likely up to
and it will see itself in you and envelope you
and though you can never leave behind starting points
it's best to continue trying.

Remember that Teutonics probably ties up
at least part of your own history
so that,
        in a way,
we've all been conquested
At least keep one eye open, peeled as they say.
When you live in the mountains a watchtower
is almost useless, and think how preposterous,
like pissing in a river and then bragging about it
or someone biting
their cheek while scarfing weisswurst.

And I wonder about rush whips as well,
though the holy ground too has scars down its back.

Thor's Oak and its petrified followers,
those who kept the body tucked in cheek
till nothing but a gob of sugars,
no one need have bothered to drive the snakes away.

*It's called winter.*

# THIS IS WORSE

*We were surprised once, long ago;*
*and now we can never be surprised again.*
—John Ashbery

We saw it from the beginning,
a predictable history on its plate
was not like the ocean recoiling
at a wave's arrival, shouldering each other sometimes
singing a tune called something like, *Just a Thought*.
He said there is no where to turn,
and this was not lost on us.
There was green smoke and there was grey smoke
and though even the small birds range,
this makes them seem less a trick
as if to say "all the variables equal one
'a nothing variance' minor heights affords."

By definition, there is no light in the dark eye:
think of this as a preface lost on the page
and you might find it useful to question
not what the words say, this much should be obvious,
but what they saw, especially in you.

This is an exercise in trying
to delete what cannot be looked at.
If there were a map it would be full
of confusing symbols, like a snakeriver
dropping ring lakes on a prairie over time.
The way is hard, and it cannot be helped.

THE SPIRAL JETTY


What was discovered that afternoon
was that the route was the real spiral,
collapsing like a slowly failing odometer.
It had seemed so significant a feature
would announce itself, would present its own
pull, like electricity running through coiled wire.

Say: Let's no longer look for houndstooth flags
as markers of a finish, or of a pattern
in nature that denotes man's touch:
when a beetle walks down a beach of sand
it leaves a long thin line
studded with small dots at left and right
as even most children know to contemplate
another's boot-tracks through the snow.

Expect no golden spikes to mark the occasion:
every moment of inquiry seems a dodge.
Our echoless whispers mimicked in the tall grass.

The dryness allowed us to escape
our own moisture, if for the moment
no one seemed able to answer
why the ice froze so softly here, why
questions like the taste of an iceberg
brought on shame as hostility, as if
at least someone should know such a thing
as the various permutations of salt and water.

Remember feeling
as though you lost the map
though it never leaves your back pocket.
Almost always, it's easier to go on foot when
six tenths is not the same as three fifths of any mile.
One learns to appreciate approximations when
even the mildest salt air of the lake can rust
a tractor through to its gears, think of your lungs.

And upon finally arriving to see it
amphibious, distended beneath a deeper melt
like a displaced mirror, I was pleased to consider
our own promontory gesture, to be able to ask
who owns a lake, and answer
the lake.

# THE NATIONAL FOUNDLING SOCIETY

Of all things left on our doorstep, this takes effort.
A new climb, the goal is not to pass off,
but to keep them like arrows in a quiver,
our skulls the rafters of a bunk-filled attic.

This is not a collage of children,
but they grew up and found their use.
We were looking for friends, not sons
or daughters, for our pints and poems.

We were the quiet sort in the backroom,
I don't know what you saw, or heard.
Of the trinkets, notes and drawings,
all that's left and found,

chanced upon children, I say keep it all.
As we kept you.

Sean Garritty has a BSc in Biology and a BA in English and Creative Writing from the University of Alberta. He completed his MFA in poetry at Brooklyn College. Sean currently works in publishing and as a freelance writer and communications consultant. He lives in Edmonton.